Minister Barb

Blessings on yo[u]
and your family. You
have been an inspiration to me'o

Love,
Rick Rammie
6/16/12

BEYOND THE GLORY OF GOD

Rick Rannie

CROSSBOOKS
PUBLISHING

CrossBooks™
A Division of LifeWay
1663 Liberty Drive
Bloomington, IN 47403
www.crossbooks.com
Phone: 1-866-879-0502

First published by CrossBooks 03/27/2012

ISBN: 978-1-4627-1496-4 (sc)
ISBN: 978-1-4627-1498-8 (hc)
ISBN: 978-1-4627-1497-1 (e)

Library of Congress Control Number: 2012904899

Printed in the United States of America

This book is printed on acid-free paper.

All Scripture references are from the King James Version of the Bible unless noted otherwise.

Preface

Have you ever experienced His glory or presence? It may have been during a praise and worship service or during a time of prayer when you felt His overwhelming love and peace. After Jesus died, He appeared to two disciples on the road to Emmaus who did not realize it was Jesus until He revealed Himself to them. They said, "Didn't our hearts burn within us as He spoke?" (Luke 24: 13-32). In that moment they experienced the presence or glory of God.

Jesus said, "And the glory which thou gavest me I have given them; that they may be one even as we are one:" (John 17:22). God wants us to experience His glory at home, work, school and church every day. The glory of God can be experienced on a continual bases and we can abide in His presence, for it is our inheritance. This book will show you how to receive and move in His glory. Walking in His glory is a great experience; however, it is only the beginning and not the end of our experience. On one hand, you must ask God to show you the full extent of His glory then you must ask Him to take you beyond the glory of God. The glory of God is the bridge that will take us to higher levels in God. It will usher us into the kingdom of God.

Acknowledgments

I thank my Lord and Savior Jesus Christ for helping me write this book. I could not have accomplished this book had it not been for my wife Patricia and my children Nicole, Benita and Jeremy. To my grandparents Marshall and Margaret Penn and Anthony and Beryl Rannie thank you. Kim and Mike DeGraphenreed, my sister and brother in-law, thank you for always encouraging me in my ministry. To all my family and friends thank you.

Joan Lisle, thank you for helping me edit this book, and James Robinson, thank you for your artwork. Thank you to all the intercessors at Unity Church of Jesus Christ, and the House of Prayer. To Diane Mixon, Sherrie Garoian, Shirley Langron, Gloria Hodgin, Joan Lisle, Keith Barry and all the others not named who have been interceding for years in State College for the glory of God and revival thank you.

To Ruth Heflin, whom I have never met personally and went on to be with the Lord, thank you, for you were at the forefront of teaching about the glory of God.

Table of Contents

Chapter 1 — The Process   1

Chapter 2 — What is the Glory of God?   9

Chapter 3 — How to Enter into Glory   23

Chapter 4 — When He Comes to Us   39

Chapter 5 — The Riches of Glory   57

Chapter 6 — Manifestations of Glory: Paul's Example   71

Chapter 7 — Don't Get Satisfied: Hezekiah's Example   81

Chapter 8 — Conclusion: Knowing You Are in the Glory of God   87

Chapter 1

THE PROCESS

Once when I was a young man I was coming home from church and the overwhelming presence of God came upon me. Since that time I had a hunger to experience the glory of God like that all the time. My question was can someone live in His presence like this every day?

Throughout the Bible, Old and New Testament, we see references made about the glory of God. How is the glory of God supposed to affect our lives? Through the Word of God and experience, I have found that the glory of God is a part of our inheritance as Christians. When I started my journey, the experience I sought was an outward experience, as Moses or Ezekiel had, in which they saw God in all His glory. I believe that God will allow us to behold Him in this way; however, to get to this level of intimacy with the Lord there are stages through which God will take us. Paul talks about going from glory to glory. God wants to do an eternal work in us where we can behold and experience His glory on a continual basis.

The glory of God is part of a three-fold process that He takes us through in order to become the sons of God who bring the Father pleasure. This process includes coming into the life of God, the glory of God, and the kingdom of God. We can see this process in Luke 9:23-27. Jesus says, "If you deny yourself and bear your cross you will find life." The life of God through the Spirit gives us power to live right. Jesus then says that those that receive his life will be those to whom He reveals His glory. He goes on to say that some of them would see the kingdom before they die. This shows we can experience the kingdom before we die. Eight days after Jesus tells them this, three of the disciples Peter, John, and James see the glory and the kingdom on the Mount of Transfiguration (Luke 9:28-36). Let us look at some definitions:

> **The Life of God** is a function of the Spirit of God within me. In Romans 8:11 we see the Spirit will quicken or give life to us. I had a vision where the Lord was at the cross and He showed me that as I received the sacrifice He made then, He would be the tree of life for me. Jesus is our life. Jesus says, "I came that you might have life and might have it more abundantly (John 10:10). Paul says, "I am crucified in Christ: nevertheless I live; yet not I, but Christ lives in me: and the life which I now live in the flesh I live by the faith of the Son of God, who loved me, and gave Himself for me." (Galatians 2:20).

> **The Glory of God** is the manifest presence of the Lord in our lives. When glory comes, we know that He is with us. This will be expanded upon in later chapters.

The Kingdom of God is receiving your inheritance as a child of God. Jesus said seek first His kingdom and His righteousness and all other things will be added to us (Matthew 6:33). My seeking the kingdom first will cause me to experience the glory, and life of God. The kingdom means realizing you are seated with Jesus in heavenly places (Ephesians 2:6). It is realizing that the Father, Jesus and all that pertains to the kingdom is inside of you (Hebrews 12:22-28). God is the kingdom. We are heirs of God and joint heirs of Jesus (Romans 8:17). So everything the Father and Jesus have is mine and this is the kingdom. The Word says, "The Lord hath prepared His throne in the heavens; and His kingdom rules over all." (Psalm 103:19). When we are seated in His throne, we are in or have His kingdom. The throne is the focal point of the kingdom.

Before the church (and we as individuals) can truly experience the kingdom of God, we must experience the life and glory of God first. Jesus said He is coming back for a glorious church without spot or wrinkle. Isaiah said, "Arise, shine for thy light has come and the glory is risen upon you" (Isaiah 60:1-2). I believe this is a call to the church for today. The following is an illustration that shows the process. David says, "Thou wilt show me the path of life: in thy presence is fullness of joy; at thy right hand there are pleasures forevermore." (Psalm 16:11). We see here that life leads to His glory, or the presence of God, which in turn leads us to His right hand. To be at His right hand, is to be in the kingdom.

In the illustration by James Robinson, the lighthouse represents Jesus, who is our life. The water is the glory, and the boat is the Holy Spirit that helps us navigate toward the kingdom. When we partake in the riches of His glory, this leads us to the sun, which is the kingdom of God. The Scripture says that Jesus is the hope of glory (Colossians 1:27). This means that Jesus is the result of the glory of God in your life.

The process: Life = The Lighthouse, The Water= The Glory of God, The Boat = The Holy Spirit, The Sun= The Kingdom.

If we look at Hebrews 12: 22-28, we see the kingdom of God described. It says:

22.

> But ye are come unto Mount Zion, and unto the city of the living God, the heavenly Jerusalem, and to an innumerable company of angels,

23.

> To the general assembly and church of the firstborn, which are written in heaven, **and to God** the Judge of all, and to the spirit, of just men made perfect.

24.

> And **to Jesus** the mediator of the new covenant, and to the **blood** of sprinkling, that speaketh better things than that of Abel.

25.

> See that ye refuse not Him that speaketh. For if they escaped not who refused Him that spake on earth, much more shall not we escape, if we turn away from Him that speaketh from heaven:

26.

> Whose voice then shook the earth: but now He hath promised, saying, Yet once more I shake not the earth only, but also heaven.

27.

*And this **word**, Yet once more, signifieth the removing of those things that are shaken, as of things that are made, that those things which cannot be shaken may remain.*

28.

Wherefore we <u>receiving</u> a kingdom which cannot be moved...

This Scripture shows that the kingdom consists of the Father, Jesus, the blood, and the Word. The kingdom consists of everything we need to have victory; this is why Jesus said, "To seek first the kingdom of God" (Matthew 6:33). Our needs are met by being in the kingdom. Revelation 12:11 says, "And they overcame him by the blood of the Lamb, and by the word of their testimony; and they loved not their lives unto the death." Because the blood and the Word are of the kingdom, this is where the overcomers dwell.

Daniel 7:14 shows us Jesus receiving dominion, glory, and a kingdom. In verse 18, Daniel prophesies about the church of the living God today. He says, "The saints of the most High shall take the kingdom, and possess the kingdom forever."

And the kingdom and dominion, and the greatness of the kingdom under the whole heaven, shall be given to the people of the saints of the most High, whose kingdom is an everlasting kingdom, and all dominions shall serve and obey Him. (Daniel 7:27)

Romans 8:17 says we are the heirs of God and joint-heirs of Christ. This means that whatever God has is mine and whatever Jesus has is mine also. If Jesus was given dominion, glory and a kingdom, then as a joint-heir, I have a right to these, too. Daniel also shows that the saints are to have dominion and enter into the kingdom as Jesus did. I John 4:17 says, "As Jesus is so are we in the earth." As mature sons and daughters, we are to walk in our kingdom authority as kings and priests before God. There are heights and depths to this that have not been touched yet. Yet today, if we as the church go after the kingdom as Jesus said, all other things will be added to us.

What about the glory of God?

> *And the glory which thou gavest me I have given them; that they may be one, even as we are one (John 17:22).*

Jesus was talking about us in this passage.

The passages in Daniel and John show that the saints of the most High have a right to the kingdom, glory and dominion. This book will deal with the glory of God. I believe that as we come into a realization of His glory, the way into the kingdom and the dominion of God will open.

Some of the questions this book will answer are:

1) What is the Word talking about when it talks of the glory of God?

2) Is it relevant for today?

3) Can each saint really experience His glory?

4) How do we enter into this experience?

If we are to be a glorious church, each individual in the body of Christ has a responsibility to receive and walk in His glory. Paul makes it clear that the kingdom and His glory belong to us.

That ye walk worthy of God, who hath called you unto His kingdom and glory (I Thessalonians 2:12).

2 Peter 1:3 also says we have been called to glory. Are you ready to answer His call to come into the glory of God, and to go beyond?

Chapter 2

WHAT IS THE GLORY OF GOD?

As a young man, the concept of the glory of God excited me. I saw what Moses, Isaiah, Ezekiel, David, Peter, and John experienced and I always believed I could have similar experiences also. Moses asked God to see His glory and God showed it to him. Isaiah saw the glory of God and he saw the Lord on His throne. Ezekiel beheld the glory of God on several occasions. The Bible says God is no respecter of persons, and that if we seek we will find, and if we knock the door will be opened to us. These men saw the glory of God, and that is what I wanted. Oh, to see His glory was my cry! This is what I sought after, and many times I was frustrated because I did not see any results. Could I really experience God like these people? What I found was that God will give us external manifestations of His glory, and He will give us visions where we can see into the spirit realm. Jesus said, "I will that they be with me where I am that they may behold my glory" (John 17:24). I have found that this can be an every day occurrence where we can behold Him in the spirit. The outward or open visions may not be as frequent, but you can experience seeing in the spirit on a continual basis. This is supposed to be the normal life for the Christian. Elisha prayed for his servant and said, "Open his eyes so he can see." Not only can we hear Him but we are also able to see Him. Our prayer must be: Lord open our eyes.

Paul talks of those who whether in body or out of body beheld things in the spirit realm. The Lord's main purpose is for us to experience and behold His glory on a continual basis. This goes beyond just having an experience but it is allowing God to do an eternal work within us.

John 17 shows that we can experience the glory of God.

22.

*And the **glory** which thou gavest me I have given them; that they may be **one,** even as we are one:*

23.

*I in them, and thou in me, that they may be made **perfect in one**; and that the world may know that thou hast sent me, and hast loved them, as thou hast loved me.*

24.

*Father, I will that they also, whom thou hast given me, be **with me where I am**; that they may **behold my glory**, which thou hast given me: for thou lovedst me before the foundation of the world.*

26.

*And I have declared unto them thy name, and will declare it: that **the love** wherewith thou hast loved me may be in them, and I in them. (my emphasis)*

(John 17:22-24 & 26)

John 17 shows us several things:

1. The glory of God is for us.
2. Glory makes us perfect in one.
3. It is Jesus' will that we be with Him.
4. It is His will that we behold His glory.
5. Love is a result of the Glory of God.

    The glory of God is love manifested.

What is the glory of God? In the Scriptures, whenever glory filled the temple, God's presence, His person, filled the temple. The definitions God gave me are as follows: Glory is as a bridge that leads us to God, or it is a tunnel that leads to God.

Glory is the vehicle He uses to bring us to Him. The glory is the manifested presence of God that we can experience in this life. When you are in someone's presence you know they are there. It is the same with God.

When we look at the Hebrew definition of glory in the <u>Strong's Concordance</u>, we see glory defined as weight. I believe this is true because it is His person that overshadows us when we come into glory. Receiving the Holy Spirit is Him in us. However, for us to be in Him, means that His being, His weight overshadows us. We will see that coming into glory is coming into perfect oneness with God. The Lord showed it to me like this; He said we are as a molecule of water in an ocean, where God is the ocean. He does not just want to be in us, but He wants us all to be in Him. His weight and all that He is comes upon us when we come into perfect oneness with God.

In Ephesians 3, God is called the Father of glory. Glory is produced by the Father, it emits from God as the rays come from the sun. Glory comes from God; it is not separate from Him. The rays of the sun are not the sun, but come from the sun and they light and warm the earth. The rays also provide energy to plants by photosynthesis. Glory is like that in the spirit realm; within glory there is life and victory for the saints. The glory of God is like also like a vast mountain range when it comes to the levels of glory that an individual can experience. People may be at different levels and have different perspectives on what the glory of God is all about. We are not to judge them, but realize they are at different places in God.

The glory of God is the manifest presence of God in your life. Coming into glory is realizing that He is there with you. It is not an end but the beginning of our walk with God. His glory is a small aspect of what He is all about, yet one can spend a lifetime experiencing the depths or the different levels of His glory. The Lord once told me to pray to know the full extent of His glory.

Examples of Glory in the Bible

Throughout the Bible, references are made about the glory of God. In Exodus 33: 11-22, we see Moses talking to God, and Moses requests that God show him the glory of God. When Moses asks to see God's glory, God shows Moses Himself in Exodus 33:22-23:

22.

And it shall come to pass, while my glory passeth by, that I will put thee in a cleft of the rock, and will cover thee with my hand while I pass by.

23.

And I will take away mine hand and thou shalt see my back part; but my face shall not be seen.

David was a man who sought after seeing the glory of God. Psalms 24:7-8 says:

7.

Lift up your heads, O ye gates; and be ye lifted up, ye everlasting door: and the King of glory shall come in.

8.

*Who is the **King of glory**? The **Lord** strong and mighty. The Lord mighty in battle.*

In Psalms 63:2, we see David's heart, He says, "To see thy power and thy *glory*, so as I have seen thee in the sanctuary."

He sought after God's glory; in fact, it was David that brought the Ark of the Covenant back to Jerusalem. The Ark was the place where the glory dwelled. If we look at the instructions God gave Moses about developing an ark and the tabernacle, we see that the tabernacle was to be a foreshadowing of the type of relationship we can have with God, as in Exodus 40: 34-35:

34.

> *Then a cloud covered the tent of the congregation, and the glory of the Lord filled the tabernacle.*

35.

> *And Moses was not able to enter into the tent of congregation because the cloud abode thereon, and the **glory of the Lord** filled the tabernacle.*

In 2 Chronicles 7:1-2, the glory of God comes and fills the temple of God to the point that the priests could not come in and minister. 1 Corinthians 3:16 says, "we are the temple of the living God," therefore we can be filled with His glory. According to Isaiah 60:7, God says, "I will glorify the house of my glory". My question is how would our churches look if God was able to fill them with glory? How would we look, the temples of God, filled and surrounded with glory?

Another example of glory in the bible is in Proverbs 3:35. It says that the wise shall inherit glory, but shame shall be the promotion of fools. When talking of wisdom in Proverbs 4:9, we see that a result of wisdom is a crown of glory.

Isaiah said he saw the Lord, and in Isaiah 6:3, he heard the angels say that the whole earth is full of His glory.

Isaiah 40:5 says:

> *And the glory of the Lord shall be revealed, and all flesh shall see it together, for the mouth of the Lord hath spoken it.*

Isaiah 60: 1 -2 says:

> *1.*
>
> *Arise, shine; for thy light is come, and and the **glory of the Lord** is risen upon thee.*
>
> *2.*
>
> *His **glory** shall be seen upon thee.*

Is his glory seen on you? When Moses came out of God's presence his face shone so that he had to put a veil on his face. The glory of the Lord was seen on him.

Isaiah 60:19 says:

> *The sun shall be no more thy light by day; neither for brightness shall the moon give light unto thee: but the Lord shall be unto thee an **everlasting light**, and thy **God thy glory**.*

Glory is what comes from God. It is as the light that comes from Him. Yet within this light we can touch God and have communion with Him. I John 1:5 says God is light.

l John 1:7 says:

> *But if we walk in the light, as He is in the light, we have fellowship one with another, and the blood of Jesus Christ His son cleanseth us from all sin.*

Another example of glory in the bible is Ezekiel 1: 26-28 which says:

26.

And above the firmament that was over their heads was the likeness of a throne, as the appearance of a sapphire stone: and upon the likeness of the throne was the likeness as the appearance of a man above it.

27.

And I saw as the color of amber as the appearance of fire round about within it, from the appearance of His loins even upward, and from the appearance of His loins even downward, I saw as it were the appearance of fire, and it had brightness round about.

28.

*As the appearance of the bow the bow that is in the cloud in the day of rain, **so was the appearance of the brightness round about. This was the appearance of the likeness of the glory of the Lord.***

When we look at Revelation, we see that John saw the same thing that Ezekiel saw.

Revelation 1:14-15 says:

14.

His head and His hairs were white like wool, as snow; and His eyes were a flame of fire.

15.

And His feet like unto fine brass, as if they burned in a furnace; and His voice as the sound of many waters. (This is what Ezekiel called the glory of God)

Let's look at what Peter, John and Paul say about the glory of God. Peter said, in I Peter 4:14, *"the spirit of glory and of God resteth upon you."* Paul said, in II Corinthians 3:18, *"But we all, with open face beholding as in a glass the glory of the Lord*, are changed into the same image from glory to glory, even as by the Spirit of the Lord." John says in Revelation 21:11, "having *the glory of God; and her light was like unto a stone most precious even like a jasper stone, clear as crystal."*

These examples were used to show that glory is not something that is separate from God. He is the Father of glory; He is the King of glory. Whenever God showed His glory He showed Himself. Glory is a manifestation of Himself to us. He uses it to show us He is with us. He was a fire by night and a cloud by day for the children of Israel. He wants to make the manifestation of Himself real to us, as it was to the children of Israel. He showed me that in glory He can take any form that He wants. In His glory He can be salvation, healing, deliverance, prosperity or whatever we need. This is why God told Moses that He is the Great I AM.

What does Jesus say about glory? Did He seek after glory? In Luke 9, we see where Peter, John and James go into the Mount of Transfiguration with Jesus.

Luke 9:32 & 34 says:

32.

But Peter and they that were with Him were heavy with sleep:
and when they were awake, ***they saw His glory,*** *and the men*
that stood with Him.

34.

While He thus spake, there came a cloud, and overshadowed them:
and they feared as they entered into the cloud. And there came a
voice out of the cloud, saying, this is my beloved Son: hear Him.

When Peter describes this scene he says in 2 Peter 1:17, "Jesus received honour and glory, when there came such a voice to Him from the excellent glory." In John 17:5, we see Jesus seeking for a higher dimension of glory, when He asks the Father for the *same glory* He had before the world was.

For individuals, John 17: 20-24 is the most significant scriptural reference to the glory of God. It says:

20.

Neither pray I for these alone, but for them also which shall
believe on me through their word;

21.

That they all may be one: as thou Father, art in me, and I in
thee, that they also may be one in us: that the world may believe
that thou hast sent me.

22.

*And the **glory** which thou gavest me I have given them; that they may be one, even as we are one.*

23.

I in them, and thou in me, that they may be made perfect in one; and that the world may know that thou hast sent me, and hast loved them, as thou hast loved me.

24.

*Father, I will that they also, whom thou hast given me, be with me where I am; that they may **behold my glory**, which thou hast given me: for thou lovedst me before the foundation of the world.*

From these Scriptures we see that Jesus sought for the glory of God for Himself. He said, "Father give me the glory I had before the foundation of the world." We also know that He walked in glory while on the earth because He said He and the Father were one.

Jesus also prayed that we receive the glory of God to be made perfect in one with Him, Him in us and we in Him. He is in us is by the baptism of the Holy Ghost. The church in some ways has gotten satisfied with this revelation and has not pressed into the glory of God which is the church in Him.

Jesus clearly states in verse 23 that the glory is for us so we can be made perfect in one. Does it not say in Ephesians that God is coming for a glorious church? The way to this is not by just receiving the baptism of the Holy Spirit but to go onto the next dimension in God which is coming into His glory.

Jesus also prayed that we have His glory, that we would be with Him where He is and behold His glory. In John 17:24, we see that this is His will for us. John 17:20 shows us that the glory of God is not just for the saints of the past but it is for us today. It is relevant for today. It says:

> *Neither pray I for these alone, but for them which*
> *shall believe on me through their word.*

From Genesis to Revelation, we see that glory is an experience God wants us to have, and it is essential to our walks with God. If you have the baptism of the Holy Ghost that is not enough. We must say: Father, what is next?

So what is the glory of God? It is the manifested presence of God made real to us. When you're in someone's presence that means they are with you. Glory allows us to realize He is with us. Glory is being in Him, which allows us to be in perfect oneness with Him. He is in us by the baptism of the Holy Spirit, and we are in Him by the cross.

Glory is the way to God. Glory is the light of God that comes from God which leads us to Him. He is the Father of glory. Glory is as a tunnel or a bridge that takes us to an intimate relationship with God.

Jesus showed us in John 17:20 that it was not just for Moses, the children of Israel, David, Solomon, Isaiah, Ezekiel, John, James, Peter and Paul to behold and experience the glory of God. The glory of God is for all of us today.

Jesus' prayer was that we be perfect in one, He in us and we in Him. This is the glory of God. This is next dimension after coming into His life.

Chapter 3

How to Enter into Glory

As I said before, for years I sought for His glory, and my motives many times were not right. I thought that with the glory of God people would accept me and my ministry would prosper. Even though I did not have any results, I knew glory was something I could obtain. God had me in John 15 for years, learning about abiding in Him. I knew that this abiding in Him would cause me to be one and I thought this was how I would experience the glory of God. My favorite Scripture during this time was Psalms 27:4:

> One thing have I desired of the Lord, that will I seek after;
> that I may dwell in the house of the Lord all the days of my
> life, to behold the beauty of the Lord, and to inquire in His
> temple.

We see in this Scripture that David sought to dwell in His house all the days of His life. I believed the result of this would cause him to behold God and to inquire or receive revelation in His temple. This

Scripture gave me hope because I knew God was not a respecter of persons.

Through my study of the Word I knew that in the Old Testament that the place where glory dwelled was in the tabernacle, in the holy of holies. In the New Testament, Jesus is the holy of holies and in order for Christians to find glory or His presence they needed to abide in Him. All of this became the foundation in my search for the glory of God. In the beginning I was seeking after an experience and what I found was Him. The Scripture is true; He is the beginning (Alpha) and end (Omega). I sought glory and found Him. When I sought His power I found He is power. He is the end of all our seeking. I also found that every true doctrine has to have the cross as its foundation. He is the beginning. If the concept of glory is true then I knew the way into it had to start with Jesus.

The Lord showed me that being one with Him came before we could behold His glory. During this time, I tried to abide which I thought was praying continually. It was after much prayer, fasting, frustration, guilt, and there was even a time I gave up on receiving the glory, that I realized that I could not bring myself into an abiding relationship with God. My cry was, "God, I can't do this!" I even heard preachers say we can't dwell continually with God. After several years of this, the Lord gave me a great revelation that changed my life. The Lord showed me I Corinthians 1:29-30,

It says:

> *29.*
>
> *That no flesh should glory in His presence.*

30.

> **But of Him are ye in Christ Jesus**, *who of God is made unto us wisdom, and righteousness, and sanctification, and redemption.*

I found that by the Father we are in Christ Jesus. This changed my life forever. It is by the Father that I have an abiding relationship with Jesus. Remember to be in Him is to have His glory and to be made perfect in one. In John 15, the Father is called the husbandman or farmer. It is the husbandman that puts the branches on the Vine, who is Jesus. Romans 11:16-23 talks about how we were grafted in the tree. But how does God do this? The answer is in verse 30; Jesus is made unto us wisdom, righteousness, sanctification and redemption. When we realize we have these spiritual blessings because of the cross, we will experience, walk and behold the glory of God. These blessings lead us to holiness. Holiness leads us to the presence of God. When I walk in holiness, I receive His image and God is able to manifest Himself to me because I am holy.

Hebrews 12: 14 says:

> *Follow peace with all men, and holiness, without which no man shall see the Lord.*

In the Old Testament, the Holy of Holies was the place in the tabernacle where God met the High Priest. It was the place where the glory came. In the New Testament times, the holy of holies is when one comes into the presence of God. When Jesus died the veil to the holy of holies was torn in two.

Psalms 15: 1-2 says:

1.

Lord who shall abide in thy tabernacle? Who shall dwell in thy holy hill?

2.

He that walketh uprightly, and worketh righteousness, and speaks the truth in His heart.

Jesus being made wisdom, righteousness, sanctification, and redemption leads us to holiness which leads us to God. When we talk about holiness today it has a bad connotation in some people's minds. Walking in holiness is not a bunch of does and don'ts but it is a glorious freedom God gives us. It allows us to be like Him.

What is holiness? It is the image of God. It is the difference between light and darkness, God being the light. It is as the difference between clean and dirty water, God being the clean water. Holiness is the image of God. When we look at Ephesians 1:4 and II Peter 1:3-4, we see that we have a right to holiness. Holiness is part of our destiny.

Ephesians 1: 3-4 says:

3.

*Blessed be the God and Father of our Lord Jesus Christ, who hath blessed us with **all spiritual blessings** in heavenly places **in Christ**.*

4.

> *According as **He hath chosen us in Him** before the foundation*
> *of the world **that we should be holy** and without blame*
> ***before Him in love**.*

We see here that we were ***chosen to be in Him*** before the foundation of the world. At the foundation of the world the Lord said, "Let's make man in our image" (Genesis 1:26). How did God make us in His image? He placed us in Jesus, that we be holy and be before Him in love. Holiness is the image of God. When Isaiah saw the glory of the Lord the angels cried, "Holy, Holy, Holy is the Lord." What a glorious destiny we have to be holy!

2 Peter 1: 3-4 says:

3.

> *According as His divine power hath given unto us **all things***
> ***that pertain unto life and godliness**, through the knowledge*
> *of Him that hath **called us to glory** and virtue.*

4.

> *Whereby are given unto us exceeding great and precious*
> *promises: that by these ye might be partakers of the **<u>divine</u>***
> ***<u>nature</u>**, having escaped the corruption that is in the world*
> *through lust.*

Peter said we have been given all things to be partakers of the divine nature. Paul in Ephesians said we have been given all spiritual blessings to be holy (Ephesians 1:3-4). If we put these Scriptures together we see that we have been given all things to have the divine nature which is holiness. We saw in Hebrews 12:14 and Ephesians 1:4, that with holiness we can see or know God, and be in Him in love and be blameless.

We have been called before the foundation of the world to be holy and be in Him. We have been called to be like God. He made us in His image.

Holiness is like a spiritual magnet in that once we embrace holiness it will draw us to God. The enemy has tried to lie to us to make us think holiness is drudgery. As a church if we embrace holiness and call it a good thing we will come into contact with the glory of God as never before. As we embrace holiness, our life becomes a song of love before the Lord.

The question then becomes, how do we come into holiness? The answer is in I Corinthians 1:30; Jesus is made unto us wisdom, righteousness, sanctification, and redemption. These are what I call the keys to intimacy with God because they all lead us to holiness.

Let's look at these keys. First of all, wisdom that comes from Jesus leads us to holiness.

Proverbs 3:35 says:

The wise inherit glory.

If wisdom leads to glory, then wisdom will lead us through holiness. Remember we are chosen to be in Him (which is glory), to be holy and without blame. Wisdom leads me to be in Him. If I were a mathematician and made an equation I could say,

Wisdom = Holiness

The next key is righteousness. Paul exhorts us to be righteous in Romans 6:19, which says:

Yield your members servants to righteousness unto holiness.

The fruit of righteousness is holiness. Therefore we can conclude that;

Righteousness = Holiness

Hebrews 10:10 and Colossians 1:22 together show us about the third key which is sanctification.

Hebrews 10:10 says:

*By the which will we are **sanctified** through the offering of the **body of Jesus** Christ once for all.*

Colossians 1:22 says:

*In the **body of His flesh** through death, to present you **holy and unblamable** and unreprovable in His sight.*

We see through these scriptures that through the offering of His body we are sanctified which allows us to be holy. Therefore we can say;

Sanctification = Holiness

We can learn about our fourth key which is redemption by looking at I Peter 1: 16-19, we see God telling us to be holy as He is holy. The scripture goes on to say that we were redeemed by the precious blood of Jesus. So to be holy we must receive that we are redeemed. We therefore make the conclusion that:

Redemption = Holiness

If we break I Corinthians 1:30, down into a mathematical equation it would be:

Wisdom + Righteousness + Sanctification + Redemption = Holiness

We are righteous because of the sacrifice of His body and blood on the cross (II Corinthians 5:21). We are sanctified by the offering of His body. We are redeemed by the shedding of His blood.

John 6:56 says:

*He that eateth my flesh, and drinketh my blood **dwelleth in me**, and I in Him.*

When I receive or eat all that is mine because of the cross (wisdom, righteousness, sanctification and redemption), then I am holy. Because I am holy I will dwell in Him, which is the glory of God, and He will dwell in me by the Holy Spirit.

Let's look at righteousness closer.

Psalm 140:13 says:

*The **upright** shall dwell in thy presence.*

Song of Solomon 1:4 says:

*The **upright** love thee.*

If we look at the entire chapter of Romans 8, it begins by showing us that there is no condemnation to them which are in Christ. The reason for this is because we are righteous because of the sacrifice of Jesus. Because of this sacrifice there is no place for guilt, because we are forgiven. The chapter ends asking the question: "What shall separate us from the love of God?" The conclusion is nothing can separate us from His love. Why is this so? It is because we are righteous. Righteousness means that there is no separation between us and God.

II Corinthians 5:21 says:

> For He hath made Him to be **sin**; that we might be made the **righteousness of God in Him**.

Righteousness means I do not have to sin. The enemy can not make me sin. But when I receive that I am righteous it is then my choice as to whether or not I sin. I am free from sin, and the fruit of this is holiness, which is having His nature. If I have His nature then it will be natural for me to be where He is at, which is in His presence.

The rights of the righteous are:

- Healing

  > Who His own self bare our sins in His own body on the tree, that we being dead to sins, should live unto **righteousness**: By whose stripes ye **were healed** (I Peter 2:24).

Because I am now righteous, I was healed at the cross. My other rights of being righteous are:

- Prosperity

  *Let them shout for joy, and be glad, that favor my **righteous** cause: yea, be magnified, which hath pleasure in the **prosperity of His servant** (Psalms 35:27).*

Psalms 112: 2-3 says:

2.

*His seed shall be mighty upon the earth: the generation of the **upright** will be **blessed**.*

3.

***Wealth and riches** shall be in his **house**: and his **righteousness** endureth forever.*

Others Scriptures pertaining to prosperity are: II Corinthians 8:9, Psalms 37:25, Psalms 84:11.

- Reign in life and no condemnation – Romans 5:17-19 and Romans 8:1.
- The presence and love of God – Psalms 15, Psalms 17:15, Psalms 23, and Song of Solomon 1:4. Psalms 140:13 says, *"**The upright shall dwell in thy presence.**"*

Sanctification is our next key to entering into the glory of God. Sanctification through the sacrifice of the body of Jesus has a couple of functions. When we are sanctified we are made clean.

John 17:17 says:

***Sanctify** them through thy truth: Thy **word** is truth.*

John 15:3 says:

> *Now ye are **clean** through the **word** which I have spoken unto you.*

When we receive the word of God that the flesh of Jesus sanctifies us (Hebrews 10:10), we are made clean. Another function of sanctification is that it removes the consciousness of sin. This means we are not conscious of, or thinking about sin or our shortcomings. What we become conscious of is the presence of God. We start to walk in the spirit and not the flesh. Another blessing of sanctification happens when we combine it with our being righteous. When these two come together confidence is birthed. This is the place of answered prayer.

I John 3:21-22 says:

> 21.
>
> *Beloved if our heart condemn us not, then we have confidence toward God.*
>
> 22.
>
> *And whatsoever we ask, we receive of Him, because we keep His commandments, and do those things that are pleasing in His sight.*

Our hearts do not condemn us when we walk in our sanctification. In this place we also know we are pleasing to God, not because of what we do, but because of receiving the sacrifice of Jesus. However, there is a perfection process we must all go through where He will perfect our hearts. During this perfection God does not want us to be in guilt or beat ourselves up. What we need to do is to ask for forgiveness and run back to the Father. I remember reading a book by Brother Lawrence, "Practicing the Presence of God." In it he said he did not dwell on his failures. When he fell he went humbly to God and asked for forgiveness. He would say, "Father if you leave me to myself I will fall." We must look to the Father to keep us from falling and bring us faultless into the presence of His glory.

Righteousness and sanctification allow me to be confident in God. Earlier I showed how we are redeemed by the blood of Jesus, which allows us to be holy or have God's nature.

If we look deeper, we see that through redemption I receive the adoption of being a son of God. I have been grafted into the Vine, who is Jesus. I am in Him; I am part of the family of God. When I receive the blood of Jesus, I become part of the bloodline of God the Father.

Galatians 4:5 says:

> To **redeem** them that were under the law, that we might receive the adoption of sons.

Galatians 4:7 says:

> Wherefore thou art no more a servant, but a son: if a son, then an heir of God through Christ.

To be a heir of God means that whatever God has is mine. I am a joint-heir with Jesus and whatever He has is mine also.

How do we come into the glory of God, the presence of God? It is by God that we are in Him, because Jesus is made unto us wisdom, righteousness, sanctification, and redemption (I Corinthians 1:30). Remember the mathematical equation:

Wisdom + Righteousness + Sanctification + Redemption = Holiness

I tried to abide and come into the presence of God of myself but I could not do it. When I realized it was by God that I was in Him this changed my life and I found myself in His presence. Paul, I believe, had the same testimony.

Philippians 3: 8-9 says:

8.

Yea doubtless, and I count all things but loss for excellency of the knowledge, of Christ Jesus my Lord: for whom I have suffered the loss of all things, and do count them but dung, that I may win Christ,

9.

And be found in Him, *not having mine own* ***righteousness,*** *which is of the law, but that, but that is which is through* ***the faith of Christ, the righteousness*** *which is of* ***God by faith.***

Paul found himself in Christ once he realized he was righteous through the righteousness which is of God by faith in Christ. Once you go through this process you too will find yourself in Him. In John 6:56,

Jesus said, "*He that eats my flesh and drinks my blood, dwells in me, and I in him.*" When we eat or receive what His blood and flesh does for us at the cross, this enables us to dwell in Him (glory), and He is in us. This has nothing to do with what we do. This is so no flesh will glory in His presence (I Corinthians 1:29). However, we like Paul must seek Him with our all. As we seek Him with our all eventually we will find Him. It is during the seeking process where He teaches us about His wisdom, righteousness, sanctification and redemption. This is the normal life. We can abide in Him, it is not impossible. We can dwell in His house all the days of our lives; it is possible to behold His glory. This is a supernatural wonder that God wants to work in all of us. Hebrew 10:19-23 sums up how we come into the presence or glory of God. Keep in mind that glory is the manifestation of God in our lives, and we are the temple of the living God.

It says:

19.

*Having therefore, brethren, boldness to enter into the holiest (**presence of God**) by the blood of Jesus (**Redemption**),*

20.

*By a new and living way, which He consecrated for us, through the veil that is to say, His flesh (**Sanctification**);*

21.

And having a high priest over the house of God;

22.

Let us draw near with a true heart in full assurance of faith, (confidence/righteousness) having our hearts sprinkled from an evil conscience, and our bodies washed with pure water (sanctification).

23.

Let us hold fast the profession of our faith without wavering: for He is faithful that promised.

This passage shows we come into the presence of God, through righteousness, sanctification and redemption. As Paul said, "Where is the boasting?" God has already done it. When wisdom, righteousness, sanctification, and redemption come together in us, they produce faith. This is the power of the gospel.

Romans 1:16-17 says:

16.

For I am not ashamed of the gospel of Christ: for it is the power of God unto salvation to every one that believeth;

17.

*For therein is the righteousness of God revealed from faith to faith: as it is written, **the just live by faith.***

Hebrews 10:38 says, "That the just live by faith and if any man draw back, my soul shall have no pleasure in him." When faith is produced I am able to stay in His presence. If I leave His presence then God is not pleased, because to depart His presence is unbelief (Hebrews 3:12).

As I receive His wisdom, righteousness, sanctification, and redemption then the way for me to abide is open to me. I can abide in Him and so can you.

The conclusion of the matter is this: We abide by faith. Faith comes by hearing and hearing by the word of God. It is through Jesus that I come to know that I am in Him and He is in me. Because of the cross, part of my inheritance is abiding with the Father and Jesus. The experience of glory is ours by faith.

Chapter 4

WHEN HE COMES TO US

As we have seen the way to glory is a two-fold process if we follow Paul's example in Philippians 3:7-10. In this passage we see that Paul was willing to suffer the loss of all things to win Christ. He was seeking after Christ this is the first process. David sought after God, He said," One thing have I desired and that will I seek after" (Psalms 27:4). The second part is realizing you are in Christ by God and Jesus is made unto us wisdom, righteousness, sanctification and redemption. These two processes develop faith; Hebrews 10:38 says, "The just live by faith."

John shows us these processes in John 14. In John 14:15, Jesus says if you love me you will keep my commandments. In verses 16-18, He talks about giving the disciples the Holy Spirit and not leaving them comfortless.

Johns 14:20 says:

> At that day ye shall know that I am in my Father, and ye in me, and I in you.

At this point you realize that He is in you and you are in Him, by the cross. In verse 21, He says," that if you keep His commandments in this place of faith or the abiding place, then you love Him." The result of this place in God is that the Father and Jesus will **manifest** themselves to you. Judas said to Jesus, "How will you manifest yourself to us and not the world?" (John 14:22).

John 14:23 says:

> *Jesus answered and said unto him, if a man love me, he will keep my words: and my Father will love him, and **we will come unto him, and make our abode with him**.*

Once there is a denial of self by you keeping His commands, the Father and Jesus promise to love and *manifest* themselves to us. This is when the glory of God comes to us. This is the glory of God being manifested in our lives. They will come to us and make their abode with us. This is beyond the baptism of the Holy Spirit. If we look at Revelation 3: 20-21, we see that there is a place in God beyond the baptism of the Holy Spirit.

Revelation 3: 20-21 says:

> 20.

> *Behold I stand at the door, and knock: if any man hear my voice, and open the door, I will come in to him and sup with him and he with me.*

21.

> *To him that overcometh will I grant to sit with me in my*
> *throne, even as I also overcame, and am set down with my*
> *Father in His throne.*

This is the same thing Jesus is saying in John 14. He will come to us when we keep His commandments. Jesus was talking to church folks in this passage in Revelation. They had the Holy Spirit, yet there was a deeper place. They got satisfied with their walk with God, because in Revelation 3:17, Jesus says, "Because you say I am rich." They thought they had arrived and there was nothing else they needed in God.

The result of the Father and Jesus coming to us is faith; we realize that He is with us. Revelation 21:3 is an example of this. It says:

> *And I heard a great voice out of heaven saying, Behold, the*
> *tabernacle of God is with men, and He will dwell with them,*
> *and they shall be His people And **God Himself shall be with***
> ***them and be their God.***

The key to this scripture is that you realize that God Himself is with you.

The Lord made this real to me in a couple of ways. The first was when He gave me a dream where the Father and Jesus were with two men. However, the men did not pay attention to the Father and Jesus. Jesus and the Father then departed from the men. God wants us to come into the realization that He is actually with us. Another illustration the Lord gave me of walking in glory was like a cloud over a mountain. I live near a mountain and one day the Lord said the glory is like that cloud over the mountain. When we are distracted from God the glory is with us but high above the mountain. Then there were times, the Lord showed me, when you are in and out of His presence and you have not learned to stay with Him. In this instance you would be a mountain where the cloud partially covers you. Then there are times when the mountain is totally covered with the cloud and the mountain cannot be seen. This place of glory is when you have the testimony of Paul and can say "I am crucified with Christ: nevertheless I live; yet not I but Christ lives in me: And the life I live in the flesh I live by the faith of the Son of God, who loved me, and gave Himself for me" (Galatians 2:20). This is a place of faith where you do not leave His presence.

The key here is that you live by the faith of the Son of God. Faith says that He is. I live by knowing God is with me. This is walking in the glory of God.

There was also a time when the Lord said that He and the Father have come to me. I said to the Lord, do I treat you like an invisible man? I received no answer. A few days later I came across Hebrews 11:27. It says:

> By faith Moses forsook Egypt, not fearing the wrath of the King: for he endured, as seeing Him who is **invisible.**

When one comes into the abiding place, and when God manifests Himself, the person comes to a place of faith. You are able to forsake the world because you know God is with you and you do not want to displease Him. Moses was able to forsake Egypt because of this faith.

Hebrews 11:6 says:

> *But without faith it is impossible to please Him for He that comes to God must believe He is, and that He is a rewarder of them that diligently seek Him.*

When glory comes you realize that He is with you. This is the key to us abiding in Him. Moses and Jesus saw the glory of God and they knew God was with them.

Exodus 34:5 says:

> *And the Lord descended in the cloud, and stood with Moses **there**, and proclaimed the name of the Lord.*

Acts 10:38 says:

> *How God anointed Jesus with the Holy Ghost and with power: Who went about doing good, and healing, all that were oppressed of the devil; **for God was with Him**.*

John 16:32 says:

> *Behold the hour cometh, yea, is now come, that ye shall be scattered, every man to his own and shall leave me alone: and yet I am not alone because the **Father is with me**.*

The key to our victory is faith. Was it not the case for Moses and Jesus? They both knew God was with them. God gives us the Holy Spirit and glory so we will be perfect in one with Him. He also gives it so we will know He is with us. This was the key to Moses' and Jesus' faith. Jesus says in John 17 that it is His will that we behold Him and be with Him where He is. If we know we are with Him, what do we have to fear? Glory causes me to know He is with me. This is faith. This is faith because faith believes that He is, or as I like to say: Faith believes He is with you.

The just or righteous live by faith, by standing on the fact that He is with us. Abiding in God is a place of faith; it is a miraculous work God does in us. Let's look at the disciples for an example of coming into the glory of God.

An Example from the Disciples

You may be reading this and say that this all sounds good, but is there an example of this process in the Bible? I believe Luke 9, gives us an example of how we come into the glory of God.

Luke 9:1-2, 6 says:

1.

    Then He called His twelve disciples together, and gave them power and authority over all devils, and cure diseases.

2.

    And He sent them to preach the Kingdom of God, and to heal the sick.

6.

    And they departed and went through the towns, preaching the gospel and healing everywhere.

Here were men that were anointed by Jesus to heal the sick and preach the kingdom of God. They preached and healed everywhere. When they came back they told Jesus what they had done. This was probably a thrilling experience for them to preach and heal the sick. These were men that people did not look up to; they were fishermen and tax collectors. However, now they moved in power and authority. This probably gave them a great boost of confidence. However, Jesus does not let them relax in their new status. He did not let them get satisfied in their new place in God. In Luke 9:18, He asks them, "Who do people say I am?" Peter answered, "Jesus is the Christ of God." In Matthew 16:17, Jesus says, "Flesh and blood has not revealed this to you, but my Father which is in heaven." The significance of these passages is that here were men who preached and healed the sick, yet they did not know Jesus, only Peter was able to answer the question. In Luke 9:23-27, Jesus proceeds to show the disciples the way to knowing Him. Romans 10:17 shows us that faith comes by hearing and hearing by the word of God. If this is the case, then Jesus had to show them the way to hearing God, to come to a place of faith.

Luke 9:23-27 says:

23.

> *And He said to them all, If any man will come after me, let him deny himself, and take up His cross daily, and follow me.*

24.

> *For whosoever will save his life shall lose it: but whosoever will loss His life for my sake, the same shall save it.*

25.

For what is a man advantaged, if He gain the whole world, and lose himself, and be cast away?

26.

For whosoever shall be ashamed of me and my words of him shall the Son of man be ashamed, when He shall come in His own glory, and in His Father's and of the holy angels.

27.

But I tell you of a truth, there be some standing here, which shall not taste of death till they see the kingdom of God.

When I used to read Luke 9:23, this Scripture would bother me, because I did not want to deny myself. The denying of self will open many doors for the church. In verse 23, Jesus is telling the disciples to deny themselves daily and to follow or seek after Him with everything they have. In verse 25, He shows them that even if they gained the world it would not be worth having an intimate relationship with Him. He then goes on and says if you are ashamed of me and my words, in this adulterous and sinful generation, of him also shall the Son of man be ashamed, when He comes in His own glory, and in His Fathers, and of the holy angels (Mark 8:38, and Luke 9:26). Jesus uses the words ashamed and adulterous together, because the spirit of adultery causes one to be ashamed of the one you are with whether a husband, wife, or

God. I John 3:15, says that if we love the world the love of God is not in us. It is that simple.

James 4:4, says:

> Ye adulterers and adulteresses, know ye not that the friendship of the world is enmity with God? Whosoever therefore will be a friend of the world is the enemy of God.

Jesus said, "if you are ashamed of me I will be ashamed of you when I come in my glory, the Father's glory and of the angel's glory". Jesus was prophesying to the disciples. He said if they deny themselves, and seek me then He will not be ashamed of them when He comes in glory. In other words, if they deny themselves and seek Him they would experience the glory of God. Jesus was not just talking about when they go to heaven but He was talking about in their lifetime. We know this because of Luke 9:27. It says:

> But I tell you of a truth, there be some standing here, which shall not taste of death, till they see the kingdom of God.

He was telling them that if they deny themselves and seek Him daily they could experience His kingdom and glory now. Daniel said he saw the saints come into the kingdom and dominion of God. Jesus was saying this experience was for now and He is saying the same thing to us today.

If we look at Hebrews 12:22-24, & 28, we see the kingdom of God described.

It says:

> 22.
>
> *But ye are come unto Mount Zion, and unto the city of the living God, the heavenly Jerusalem, and to an innumerable company of angels,*
>
> 23.
>
> *To the general assembly and church of the firstborn, which are written in heaven,* **and to God** *the Judge of all, and to the spirit, of just men made perfect.*
>
> 24.
>
> *And to Jesus the mediator of the new covenant, and to the blood of sprinkling, that speaketh better things than that of Abel.*
>
> 28.
>
> ***Wherefore we <u>receiving</u> a kingdom which cannot be moved.***

Coming into the kingdom is coming to a place in God where the Father and Jesus are manifested to you, and you are living in a state where this is your daily experience. This is possible for you. John 14:21 says, "He that hath my commandments, and keepeth them, he it is that loveth me (not ashamed of Him), and he that loveth and shall be loved of my Father, and I will love Him, ***and will manifest myself to him***".

John 14:23 says, "We will come unto him and make our abode with him." We enter into the kingdom when they come to us. How do they come to us? Jesus said, "When I come in my glory, my Father's glory and the angel's glory" (Luke 9:26). Glory is as a tunnel, bridge that leads us to God. As I walk in glory, I become a partaker of the kingdom of God. The glory and the kingdom are not separate. Revelation 21: 10-11 and Hebrews 12:22 both talk about the heavenly or the holy Jerusalem. In Revelation the holy Jerusalem is called the bride of Christ. This is the kingdom of God, and we see in Revelation 21:11 that this kingdom has the glory of God as her light. The Lord showed me that His people are His kingdom. When He comes to us then we are partakers of His glory and kingdom. Some do not partake in this experience because the kingdom of God is taken by force. We are told to seek first the kingdom and all else will be added to us (Matthew 6:33). What is the kingdom? It is the Father and Jesus coming to us, and staying or abiding in Him by faith. The Kingdom of Heaven is our inheritance. The kingdom is sitting with them in their throne in the heavenlies.

Glory is like the clothes that God wears. Psalms 91:1 says that, "He that dwells in the secret place of the most High shall abide under the shadow of the Almighty." Our shadows are dark but He has a shadow of light and life. The glory, kingdom and power are not separate entities, but when we touch glory we touch them all.

Matthew 6:13 says, "Thine is the kingdom, power and glory." In other words, He is the kingdom, power and glory. Jesus told the disciples they would see the kingdom and glory, and they saw Jesus and the Father in glory.

I Corinthians 1:24 says, "Christ is the power of God." When Moses asked God to show him glory, God showed Moses Himself. God is the Father of glory (Ephesians 1:17). Jesus said the kingdom is likened to a land owner who leaves his land to people to watch. The land owner comes back and rewards the laborers according to their work. He is the landowner who comes back to us (Matthew 25:14-30). Jesus and the Father are the focus of the kingdom, because all authority and power belong to them.

Jesus wanted the disciples to go beyond the power and authority they received, and come into the glory and the kingdom of God. He wanted them to come into the fullness of God. The Scripture says eight days later after He said deny yourselves Jesus took Peter, John and James up into a mountain to pray. In Luke 9:31, they saw Moses and Elijah appear with Jesus in glory. Luke 9:32 says they saw His glory. Did not Jesus say if they denied themselves and were not ashamed of Him they would experience glory?

In Luke 9:34-35, it says, "While He thus spoke, there came a cloud, and overshadowed them: and they feared as they entered into the cloud. And there came a voice out of the cloud saying, this is my beloved Son hear Him. At this point Peter, John and James saw the glory of God and God declared Jesus was His Son. In 2 Peter 1:16, Peter describes this experience as being eyewitnesses of His majesty or royalty. It was at his point they saw the Father and Son together and what they saw was the kingdom of God. The Father told them to hear Him and to be obedient. At this point Peter, John and James experience the glory, the kingdom and the dominion. They realize Jesus is the fullness of God. He is the kingdom, power and glory of God. He is the end of our seeking.

The previous passage shows that the denial of self is not to be drudgery but a blessing. Faith says He is and is a rewarder of them that diligently seek Him. The reward of denial is glory and the kingdom of God. Isn't that a blessing?

When they came out of the mountain they came to the other disciples who could not heal a boy with an unclean spirit. Jesus heals the boy and the disciples want to know why they could not. Jesus calls them faithless and perverse (Luke 9:41).

How could they be faithless? Here were men of power and authority that healed all. Yet Jesus said they were faithless. They were faithless because faith believes that He is. Faith comes by hearing and hearing by the word of God. Remember Jesus told them to deny themselves and follow or seek Him to come into the glory and kingdom of God. These disciples were not there to hear God say this is my son. They were perverse because they were satisfied with the power and authority they had and did not seek Jesus on a deeper level. They were perverse because they loved the world more. They loved the praise of men more. In Acts 3:16, Jesus healed through Peter. The first thing Peter says to the people is why do you look on us as if we did this? They learned from the mountain experience that they could do nothing of themselves.

The disciples said why could we not heal and Jesus said because of unbelief. What is unbelief? Hebrews 3:12, says, "Take heed, brethren, lest there be in any of you an evil heart of unbelief, ***in departing from the living God.***" Leaving His presence is moving in unbelief.

Matthew 17:20 says:

> *And Jesus said unto them, Because of your unbelief: for verily I say unto you, If ye have faith as a grain of mustard seed, ye shall say unto this mountain, Remove here to yonder place; and it shall remove, and nothing shall be impossible unto you.*

If we know just a little bit that He is with us we can move mountains. Remember faith says He is with me. Hebrews 11:1 says, "Now faith is the substance of things hoped for, the evidence of things not seen." Many times the focus of this Scripture is to see how faith can get my prayers answered. However, the focus of faith, the focus of this Scripture is Jesus. Jesus is the substance of things hoped for. I Timothy 1:1 says, "Jesus Christ is our hope." Faith is the evidence of things not seen. The evidence of things not seen is the cross. The cross is the foundation of our faith. When Jesus is the focus of our faith, then we will believe. Hebrews 11:6:

> *But without faith it is impossible to please Him: for he that comes to God must believe that He is, and that He is a rewarder of them that diligently seek Him.*

I used to think that God would reward me with things if I diligently sought Him. I then realized that if I diligently sought Jesus I would be rewarded by finding Him. I would then walk in faith because I would know Jesus is with me. This is what Paul meant in Galatians 2:20:

I am crucified in Christ: nevertheless I live; yet not I, but Christ lives in me: and the life which I now live in the flesh I live by the faith of the Son of God, who loved me, and gave Himself for me.

After Jesus teaches the disciples about unbelief, He gives them another tool to fight the enemy. Matthew 17:21 says, "Howbeit this kind goeth not out but by prayer and fasting. He did not tell them to fast and pray to cast out that type of demon. Fasting and prayer was to bring them to a higher level of faith.

Isaiah 58:6 & 8 says:

6.

Is not this the fast that I have chosen? To loose the bands of wickedness, to undo the heavy burdens, and to let the oppressed go free, and ye break every yoke?

8.

*Then shall thy light break forth as the morning, and thine health shall spring forth speedily: and thy righteousness shall go before thee; the glory **of the Lord shall be thy reward.***

Fasting and prayer brings us to righteousness and the glory of God. We will then see the mountains in our lives move, because we know He is with us. Psalms 97:5 says, "The mountains melt at the presence of God."

Denying yourself, prayer, fasting and seeking Him will lead us to the glory, the kingdom and the power of God. Isn't this what Daniel saw? It is for the saints to inherit the kingdom, power and glory of God.

The Lord showed me that He wants to heal the blind, the deaf, and all manner of sickness and disease. However, He is limited because of the level of glory we are at. The greater the levels of glory you are at the closer to God you are. Each level of glory has a corresponding level of power. The disciples had power yet there was a higher place for them to reach, which comes by fasting and prayer.

An Example from Paul

Let's now look at the example of Paul in Philippians 3:7-10, keeping in mind the Luke 9 example of the disciples. Paul said, "That he suffered the loss of all things to win Christ." He was willing to lose all things. He was willing to deny himself and to bear his cross. In Galatians 2:20, he says, "I have been crucified with Christ: nevertheless I live; yet not I, but Christ lives in me: and the life which I live in the flesh I live by the faith of the Son of God." This Scripture also shows Paul denied himself and bore his cross. The result of this was that he found Christ in him. He found himself in the glory or the presence of God. Paul says it was not because of his righteousness. It was not because of his ability to do things right, but because of the righteousness which is of God by faith. The results of coming into glory are seen in Philippians 3:10, which are to know Him, the power of His resurrection, and the fellowship of His sufferings being made conformable to His death.

Has He come to you? Have you come into glory yet? The way has been made for us. Let's review: We are in Jesus by God, who is made unto us wisdom, righteousness, sanctification, and redemption. By the cross we have a right to His presence. As we receive these by faith the fruit is holiness. Love causes me to stay in His presence. As I deny myself and bear my cross daily, God will bring me into His glory, kingdom and power.

The Word says in Matthew 11:12, the kingdom suffereth violence, and the violent take it by force. When God brought me into glory the way was made for His kingdom and power to come into my life. God wants to do the same for you.

Chapter 5

THE RICHES OF GLORY

When people come into glory they will find that there are benefits to walking in His glory.

Psalms 16:11 says:

> *Thou wilt show me the path of life: In thy presence is fullness of joy; at thy right hand there are pleasures forevermore.*

Paul talks about the riches of glory in Ephesians 3:16-21:

16.

> *That He would grant you, according to the riches of His glory, to be strengthened with might by His Spirit in the inner man;*

17.

> *That Christ may dwell in your hearts; that ye, being **rooted and grounded in love**,*

18.

May be able to comprehend with all saints what is the breadth, and length, and depth, and height;

19.

*And to know the love of Christ, which passeth knowledge, that ye might be filled with all the fullness **of God**.*

20.

Now unto Him that is able to do exceeding abundantly above all that we ask or think, according to the power that worketh in us.

21.

Unto Him be glory in the church by Christ Jesus, throughout all ages, world without end. Amen.

One of the benefits of His glory is that God strengthens us with His might. Revelation 4:5 talks about the seven spirits of God that are before the throne of God. Isaiah 11:2, talking about Jesus, says:

> *And the spirit of the Lord shall rest upon Him, the **spirit of wisdom** and **understanding**, the **spirit** of counsel and might, the spirit of knowledge and of **the fear of the Lord**.*

One of the seven spirits Jesus had was the spirit of might. Paul says in Ephesians 6:10, "Finally, my brethren, be strong in the Lord, and in the power of His might." There is a might that comes to us from the glory of God. This is so that when we have to go through warfare we have the strength we need to be victorious. Isaiah 40:10 says, "Behold the Lord will come with a strong hand." God wants to anoint us with His might. In the context of Ephesians 3:16, we are given might so that Christ can dwell in our hearts, by faith. This might is strength to stay in the presence of the Lord.

The next benefit of glory is that Christ dwells in our hearts by faith that we be rooted and grounded in love. Christ in us by faith was Paul's way to describe how we experience Christ and the kingdom in the spirit realm. It is like hearing in the spirit. You do not hear him in the natural, even though you could, but you hear Him most of the time in the spirit or within you. This is beyond the Holy Spirit being in us. The Holy Spirit's purpose is to lead us to all truth. Jesus is truth. Christ in us is when the Father and Jesus come and make their abode with us. It is here that we can experience Jesus, the Father and the kingdom within us. Paul said, "For now we see through a glass, darkly; but then face to face: now I know in part; but then shall I know even as also I am known" (I Corinthians 13:12). This is the place of seeing in the spirit, and experiencing the kingdom daily. We also come to realize that love or the heart of God is within us.

This is what Jesus was talking about in John 17:24:

24.

> *Father I will that they also, whom thou hast given me, be with me where I am; that they may behold my glory, which thou hast given me: for thou lovedst me before the foundation of the world.*

The way the Father does this is seen in John 17:26:

26.

> *That the love where with thou hast loved me may be in them,*
> *and I in them.*

Ephesians 1:4 says we are chosen in Christ before the foundation of the world so that we should be holy and before Him in love. So by Christ being in us and we being in Him we are rooted and grounded in love. The glory of God is love manifested, in that we are taken into the heart of God. This is the place that Jesus prepared for us. This is what Jesus was talking about when He said in my Father's house are many mansions (John 14:2). Psalm 91 says whoever dwells in the secret place of the most high will abide under His shadow. The Song of Solomon 2:3-4, says, "I sat down under His shadow with great delight, and His fruit was sweet to my taste. He brought me to the banqueting house, and His banner over me was love." When I am under His shadow I am in the secret place. The secret place is the banqueting house, it is His heart, and it is love.

Realizing Christ is in us causes us to come into the heart of God. Ephesians 3:18 talks of knowing the breadth, and length, and depth and height of love, these terms are terms of measurement for a building. Ezekiel was told to measure the breadth, length and height of the temple. So this verse, is talking about the temple of God, the heart of God, the Holy of Holies. Hebrews 10:19-21 says:

19.

> *Having therefore, brethren, boldness to enter into the holiest*
> *by the blood of Jesus,*

20.

By a new and living way which He hath consecrated for us, through the veil, that is to say, his flesh;

21.

And having a high priest over the house of God;

Throughout the Bible there are references made about a dwelling place for us to experience in the spirit realm. It is a place called love. Below is a list of these:

- *The secret place. (Psalm 91:1)*
- *The tabernacle, the holy hill. (Psalm 15:1)*
- *The house of God. (Psalm 23:6)*
- *That I may dwell in the house of the Lord. (Psalm 27:4)*
- *God dwells in the high and holy place. (Isaiah 57:15)*
- *Thy habitation. (Psalm 91:9)*
- *Our dwelling place in all generations. (Psalm 90:1)*
- *Strong habitation. (Psalm 71:3)*
- *In my Father's house are many mansions: if it were not so, I would have told you. I go to prepare a place for you. (John 14:2)*
- *Made a pillar in the temple of God. (Revelation 3:12)*
- *No temple, for the Lord God Almighty and the Lamb are the temple of it. (Revelation 21:22)*
- *He that dwells in love dwells in God and God in him. (I John 4: 15-16)*

When we look at the above Scriptures we can assume that there is a dwelling place we can experience as Christians. This is not a place we can only experience when we die and go to heaven, but it is a place we can experience now. It is the place of rest spoken about in Hebrews 3 and 4. David prayed that he would dwell in His house all the days of his life (Psalms 27:4).

The foundation of the riches of glory is to know the love of God. Knowing His love is our greatest treasure. This love is the heart of God, it is our dwelling place.

It is through the blood and flesh of Jesus and He being in us that, we can come into the heart of God, the love of God, and the Holy of Holies. This is because Jesus dwells in love, and He brings us to the place called love (Song of Solomon 2:4).

Revelation 3:12 says:

12.

He that overcometh will I make a pillar in the temple of my God, and he shall go no more out: and I will write upon him the name of my God, and the name of the city of my God, which is new Jerusalem, which cometh down out of heaven from my God: and I will write upon him my new name.

Once I come to know love, Ephesians 3:19 says, I will come to know the fullness of God. Not only do I know that Jesus is in me but I know the fullness of God or God Himself is in me. Revelations 21:3 says:

> *Behold the tabernacle of God is with men, and He will dwell with them, and they shall be his people, and God himself shall be with them, and be their God.*

II Chronicles 7:14-16, shows that if we seek His face, the Lord will give us His ears, eyes and heart. When I have someone's ears, and eyes I have their face. In I Peter 3:12, it says that the Lord's eyes are on the righteous and His ears are attentive to their prayer. But His face, eyes, and ears, are against those that do evil. When we walk in righteousness we have His fullness in us.

The fullness of God is to know that because of love we are heirs of God and joint-heirs with Christ. Whatever God the Father and Jesus have is mine. The Father is my inheritance.

Paul says in Colossians 2:9-10:

> *9.*
>
> *For in Him dwelleth all the fullness of the Godhead bodily.*
>
> *10.*
>
> *And ye are complete in Him, which is the head of all principality and power.*

Daniel says of Jesus, in Daniel 7:14:

> *And there was given Him dominion, and glory, and a kingdom.*

Daniel 7:27 says:

> *And the kingdom and dominion, and the greatness of the kingdom under the whole heaven, shall be given to the people of the saints of the most High, whose Kingdom is an everlasting Kingdom, and all dominions shall serve and obey Him.*

When I come to know love then I will know that glory, the kingdom and dominion belong to me. This is all because of the riches of His glory.

Another benefit is to know that He is able to do all we ask or think according to the power that works in us. This is what Jesus meant when He said in John 15:7, "If ye abide in me, and my words abide in you, ye shall ask what ye will and it shall be done unto you." When righteousness and sanctification come together then confidence is birthed and you can ask what you will. This is a place of trust and love, because you are asking what you will and you do not want to do anything against the Fathers will. Jesus was in this place of trust with the Father because in John 17:24, He says, "*I will* that they be with me and behold my glory."

The final benefit in Ephesians 3 is for the church in Ephesians 3:21,

> *Unto Him be glory in the church by Christ Jesus throughout all ages, world without end. Amen*

Glory in the church is **Revival, Revival, and Revival.** God does not just want to touch individuals with glory but He wants glory in the church. Jesus said He is coming back for a glorious church without spot or wrinkle (Ephesians 5:27).

Revival is the glory of God manifested in our homes, churches, cities, and nations. Revivals have died because we have looked at them as being the end of our seeking. We are told to seek after the kingdom. When we do this God will bring us to glory because glory is the vehicle that leads us to God and the kingdom. Revival or glory in the church is the beginning of us walking in the kingdom of God. The kingdom of God is walking with a consciousness or a knowing that the Father and Jesus are with you continually. In order for revival or glory to be in the church it is something we must seek after. Revival is not the end, it helps usher us into the kingdom of God.

Hosea 6:1-3 says:

1.

Come, and let us return unto the Lord; for He hath torn, and He will heal us; He hath smitten, and He will bind us up.

2.

After two days will He revive us; in the third day He will raise us up, and **we shall live in His sight.**

3.

Then shall we know, if we follow on to know the Lord: His going forth is prepared as the morning; and He shall come unto us as the rain, as the latter and former rain unto the earth.

In Hosea 6:1-3, we see that God promises to revive them, raise them up and live in His sight. The results of revival are in verse three; we will know Him and He will come to us. This scripture shows that revival is coming into the glory of God.

If we look in I Chronicles 13, we see that David wanted to bring the ark of God back to Israel. The ark of God represented the glory of God for the children of Israel. God would overshadow the ark with His glory. When David tried to bring the ark to Jerusalem they placed it on a cart and praised the Lord as they brought it back. When the cart became unsteady a man named Uzza tried to keep it from falling, but God became angry and killed Uzza. I Chronicles 15:13, shows that God killed Uzza because they did not seek Him according to His strategy for bringing the glory to Jerusalem.

When David saw Uzza was killed he sent the ark to home of Obededom.

I Chronicles 13:14 says:

> And the ark of God remained with the family of Obededom in his house three months. And the Lord blessed Obededom, and all that he had.

When David saw Obededom being blessed he brought the ark to Israel using God's strategy. Revival is the manifestation of glory in our churches, cities and nations. God will touch an individual and use that person to touch nations. Glory will cause the kingdom and dominion to be established in individuals, cities, and nations. Paul said we go from glory to glory. So if you are seeking for revival in your church you must ask for His strategy. There are times He comes and we do not recognize Him, and miss our time of visitation (Luke 19:44).

There have been times when God said revival has come to our local church, but because it does not look like revival in other places as Toronto or Pensacola some felt revival is was not there. However, God will take a congregation from glory to glory. God wants glory to come to the church so we can corporately experience the riches of His glory. Our victory is being in Him.

Look at the temple that Solomon built. Glory came to the temple, and 2 Chronicles 7:2 says," the ministers could not minister because the glory cloud filled the Lord's house." God was there and He gave them several promises (II Chronicles 7:12-18):

1. *If drought would come He would deliver if they humble themselves, pray, seek His face and turn from their wicked ways.*

2. *He would hear them, forgive them and heal them.*

3. *His eyes would be open and ears attent to their prayer.*

4. *He would choose and sanctify them so they would have His name.*

5. *His eyes and heart would be with them perpetually (which means from sunrise to sunset).*

6. *He would establish the throne of thy kingdom. God was talking to Solomon but this applies to us also. A benefit of glory is that we are brought into the kingdom.*

All of these promises are riches of His glory.

II Chronicles 7: 1-2 says:

> *The glory of the Lord filled the house. And the priests could not enter into the house of the Lord, because the glory of the Lord had filled the Lord's house.*

Has the glory of the Lord filled the Lord's house where you worship? Is God a respecter of persons, does God have favorites? I believe it is God's will for His glory to fill the earth; therefore it is His will for His glory to fill your churches. We have Ephesians 3:21 as a promise.

Ephesians 3:21 says;

> *Unto Him or (By God the Father), be glory in the church by Christ Jesus (Jesus is made unto us wisdom, righteousness, sanctification, and redemption) throughout all ages, world without end Amen.*

Several years ago God gave me a vision where every state in the United States had the glory of God in them. Revival belongs to us because of Christ Jesus.

Another result of glory is prosperity. In II Samuel 6:11, it says that when the ark of the Lord was at Obededom's house for 3 months, the Lord blessed Obededom and his entire household.

Philippians 4:19 says:

> *But my God shall supply all your need according to His **riches in glory** by Christ Jesus.*

We have a promise that God will supply all our need according to His riches in glory. This is why in Matthew, Jesus says take no thought of what to eat or drink but to seek first the kingdom and His righteousness and all other things will be added to you (Matthew 6:33). The glory of God leads us to the kingdom and our needs are meet.

Another benefit of glory is joy. Walking with God is not boring but in His presence is fullness of joy and at His right hand are pleasures for evermore (Psalms 16:11).

John 15:10-11 says:

10.

If ye keep my commandments, ye shall abide in my love; even as I have kept my Father's commandments, and abide in His love.

11.

These things have I spoken unto you that my joy might remain in you, and that your joy might be full.

In Hebrews we see that when we walk in faith we please God. Faith says He is with me. The way we abide in Him is by faith and we believe He is with us and do not sin. One day the Lord told me to give Him my sadness, and receive His joy. He said know that He is there when all others may leave us. One of Jesus' purposes is seen in Isaiah 61:3: To give the oil of joy for mourning. One of God's promises in Isaiah 56:7 says," that God will bring us to His holy mountain, and make us joyful in His house of prayer." There were times when I found prayer to be boring. When I asked God to make me joyful in prayer, God changed my prayer life. It is now one of the most exciting things I do.

It is time for the church to tap into the ***riches of the glory of God***. Ask God to show you the full extent of His glory.

Chapter 6

MANIFESTATIONS OF GLORY: PAUL'S EXAMPLE

When we look at Paul's life he gives us an example of how glory affects one's life. Paul gives us an example of the manifestation of glory in his life in Philippians 3:7-11.

Philippians 3: 7-11 says:

7.

> *But what things were gain to me, those I counted loss for Christ.*

8.

> *Yea doubtless, and I count all things but loss for the excellency of the knowledge of Christ Jesus my Lord: for whom I have suffered the loss of all things and do count them but dung, that I may win Christ,*

9.

And be found in Him, not having mine own righteousness, which is of the law, but that which is through the faith of Christ, the righteousness which is of God by faith.

10.

That I may know Him, and the power of His resurrection, and the fellowship of His sufferings, being made conformable unto His death;

11.

If by any means I might attain unto the resurrection of the dead.

In Luke, we saw Jesus tell the disciples to deny themselves and follow Him. The result was glory and the kingdom of God being manifested to them. We see the same thing here in this passage in Philippians. The result of Paul denying himself brought him to a place where he was in Christ. As we saw before this means he was in glory, he was abiding in Him. The result or manifestation of glory causes three things to happen. They are:

1. To know Him
2. To know the power of resurrection
3. To know the fellowship of His sufferings

Let's look at these three separately. You may wonder how is knowing Him a result of glory. The following Scriptures will give us some insight into this.

I Corinthians 13:9-12 says:

9.

For we know in part, and we prophesy in part.

10.

But when that which is perfect is come (Jesus), then that which is in part shall be done away.

11.

When I was a child, I spake as a child, I understood as a child, I thought as a child: but when I became a man I put away childish things.

12.

*For now we see through a glass, darkly; but then face to face: now I know in part; but then shall I know even **as also I am known**.*

2 Corinthians 3:18 says:

But we all with open face beholding as in a glass the glory of the Lord, are changed into the same image from glory to glory, even as by the Spirit of the Lord.

In Luke 9:23, Jesus says if you deny yourself, He will come to you in His glory.

I Corinthians 13:10 says, "When that which is perfect is come (which means when Jesus comes), that which was in part will be done away.

In chapter 13, Paul is talking about a better way than having the gifts. He is talking about the love of God. You can be anointed to move mountains, and do all sorts of things through your gifting. However, if we are not moving in love, the gifting alone is not what it should be. Without love we minister in part. In verse 11, when we are as children in the spirit we understand and think as a child. When we become mature in the spirit we put aside the childish things. The childish things in this passage are the gifts of the spirit, because when I realize He that is perfect is with me then I do not move in part anymore. I realize that it is Jesus that is doing the work. Jesus says in John 14:10, "The words I speak to you, I do not speak myself: but it is the Father that dwells in me, He does the works." It is the same for us.

In verse 12, we see that when He comes there is a seeing in the spirit that occurs. Paul said it is like looking in a glass darkly, but then face to face I will know Him as I am known. He does not know in part anymore.

2 Corinthians 3:18 says: "As I behold in a glass the glory of God I am changed into the same image from glory to glory". There is a progression that happens. When the spirit comes in us as prophesized in Acts 2:17-19, then we are to see visions and dreams. We have a mandate or it is part of our purpose to see in the spirit. There is a seeing in the spirit that every Christian should experience. Jesus prayed that we would be where He is and that we behold His glory (John 17). God does not just want us to hear him. He said His sheep know His voice, but He also

wants us to behold His glory. Have you ever seen blind sheep? We are to hear and see in the spirit.

As Paul says in I Corinthians 13, when you begin seeing in the spirit it is as looking in a glass darkly. However, as we progress in this you will go from glory to glory, and you will come to a point when you are face to face with Him as Moses was. When I am face to face I will know Him as I am known.

I John 3:6 says:

> *Whosoever abideth in Him (the place of glory) sinneth not: whosoever sinneth hath not seen **Him**, neither **known Him**.*

Seeing Him is the beginning of knowing Him, and this is for all the saints of God.

2 Corinthians 3:18, says," **But we all**, with open face beholding as in a glass the glory of the Lord." Beholding Him is not a once in awhile experience but it can be a daily experience as we learn to dwell in His presence.

Jude 1:20-21 says:

20.

> *But ye, beloved, building up yourselves on your most holy faith, praying in the Holy Ghost,*

21.

> *Keep yourselves in the love of God, looking for the mercy of our Lord Jesus Christ unto eternal life.*

Philippians 3:20-21 says:

20.

For our conversation is in heaven from whence also we look for the Savior, the Lord Jesus Christ.

21.

Who shall change our vile body, that it may be fashioned like unto His glorious body, according to the working whereby He is able even to subdue all things unto Himself.

I find the passage in Jude to be very interesting. First of all we are encouraged to build up our faith by praying in the Holy Spirit. Faith says that He is with us. If I know He is with me then I have to understand that He wants to hear His language. Speaking in tongues is the language of the kingdom of God. We are told to build up our faith by praying in the spirit. Why is this? In Romans 8, it says that the spirit makes intercession for us according to the will of God. This act builds up my faith and it keeps me in the love of God according to Jude 21. If I am in the love of God I am in His presence and I am keeping His commands. I John 3:24 says, "if I keep His commands then I know I am abiding with Him." Jude 1:21 goes on to say, "Looking for the mercy of our Lord Jesus Christ." When you combine this scripture with Philippians 3:20, which says, "For our conversation is in heaven from whence also we look for the savior, the Lord Jesus Christ. The result is that when I pray in the spirit or have conversation in heaven, I am to *look* or see Jesus Christ in the spirit realm.

Paul says in I Corinthians 13:10-12 that "when He comes, *now we see* through a glass darkly: but then face to face: now I know in part; but then shall know even as also I am known." Paul is not talking about when we go to heaven but he said *now we see*. God does not just want us to hear Him but to see Him. Jesus heard and saw the Father. Jesus said I do only what I see the Father doing (John 5:19).

Jesus said, "I will that they be with me where I am to behold my glory." This is so we can know Him. This is not a fantasy but a reality every saint can experience. David's desire was to dwell in His house all the days of his life **to behold** His beauty and inquire in His temple.

Paul also said that he came into His presence not just to know Him but he also wanted to know the power of His resurrection. The Lord stated to me that He wants to heal the blind, deaf and all manner of sickness and disease through us. However, He is hindered in moving through us because His people have only reached certain levels of glory. He said for every level of glory there is a corresponding level of power.

Isaiah 40:10 says:

> *Behold the Lord will come with power, and His arm shall rule for Him; behold, His reward is with Him and His work before Him.*

When God comes He brings His power with Him. I Corinthians 1:24 says that Jesus is the power of God. The key to having power is being in His glory.

Psalms 97:5 says:

> *The hills melted like wax at the presence of the Lord, at the presence of the Lord, at the presence of the Lord of the whole earth.*

Jesus said if we have faith as a grain of a mustard seed we will say to the mountain be removed and it will go into the sea. Faith is to know He is with me. I have this knowledge when I am in His glory. Jesus says if we abide in Him and His word abides in us we can ask what we will. This is moving in the power of God. If we look at how Jesus was successful in ministry, then we will have a road map on how to move in ministry.

Acts 10:38 says:

> *How God anointed Jesus of Nazareth with the Holy Ghost and with power: who went about doing good, and healing all that were oppressed of the devil;* **for God was with Him.**

Jesus said He did nothing of Himself. In this Scripture we see that He was anointed with the Holy Ghost and power but that was not enough for Jesus. He was successful because of the last part of this verse it says, **God was with Him.** This was the key to His power. If we look at Mark 16:20, we see the key to the apostles power.

Mark 16:20 says:

> *And they went forth, and preached every where, the Lord working with them, and confirming the word with signs following. Amen.*

Jesus had died, arose from the dead and went to heaven, and yet we see He had come to them and was working with them. Knowing God was with them was the key to their power, which came by being in glory.

We see this again in Acts 4:10, where Peter and John pray for a lame man's healing.

It says:

> *Be it known unto you all, and to all the people of Israel, that by the name of Jesus Christ of Nazareth, whom ye crucified, whom God raised from the dead, even by Him doth this man stand here before you whole.*

The way to doing the greater works is in His glory.

The third result of glory Paul talks about in Philippians is the fellowship of His sufferings. This is the embracing of denying yourself and bearing your cross daily.

Romans 8:18 says:

> *For I reckon that the sufferings of this present time are not to be compared with the **glory** which shall be revealed in us.*

As we saw in Luke 9, the result of the disciples denying themselves and following Jesus was to come into glory and the kingdom. The Lord also showed me that the fellowship of His sufferings is to take up the mantle of ministry. It is doing the work of God on the earth. Jesus said, "If they persecuted me, they will persecute you" (John 15:20). The way will not always be easy but we have the assurance that the Lord is always with us

The manifestations of glory in Paul's life led him to know God, know His resurrection power, and know the fellowship of His sufferings. Glory acted as a bridge to bring Paul to the Father and Jesus.

Chapter 7

Don't Get Satisfied: Hezekiah's Example

God says that if we seek Him we will find Him. The question we must ask is what do you do when you find Him? In Deuteronomy 6:12, God warns the children of Israel about not forgetting Him, once He prospered them. We have to watch out for the same thing. We can not get satisfied with a revelation we received yesterday. We must always be asking God what is next. The revivals in the past stopped because I believe that this question was not asked. The life of Hezekiah is an example of the dangers of becoming complacent or satisfied with your present situation or revelation.

2 Kings 18:5-7 says of Hezekiah:

5.

He trusted in the Lord God of Israel, so that after him was none like him among all the kings of Judah, nor any that were before him.

6.

*For **he** cleaved to the Lord, and departed not from following Him, but kept His commandments,*

7.

***And the Lord** was with him; and He prospered whithersoever he went forth; and he rebelled against the king of Assyria, and served him not.*

Hezekiah's life is another example of what happens to you when you walk in glory. As we see it is written that he was the greatest King of Judah. There was no king before him or after him that was greater because he departed not from God. His lineage included King David. So in God's sight Hezekiah was greater than David. David is called Hezekiah's father. David was known as one who was after God's heart, and it was David who wanted to dwell with God all his days.

Hezekiah had a great testimony. It was a testimony that many today would want as their own. I would want it said of myself that I cleaved to the Lord, and departed not from following Him.

The never departing from God denotes an abiding relationship with God as seen in John 15. This is the place of glory where we are fruitful, our prayers are answered and we are walking in love. We can conclude then that Hezekiah was in a good place in God. He was in glory because 2 Kings 18:7 says the Lord was with him. Hezekiah was in a good place; however, if we look at his life we see that God wanted Him to go beyond his testimony.

In 2 Kings 18 & 19, we see where the King of Assyria came against Judah. The King of Assyria mocked God and tried to get the people of Judah to go against Hezekiah. In this situation Hezekiah prays and God sends a message through Isaiah.

2 Kings 19:6-7 says:

6.

And Isaiah said unto them thus shall ye say to your master, thus saith the Lord, Be not afraid of the words which the servants of the King of Assyria have blasphemed me.

7.

Behold I will send a blast upon him, and he shall hear a rumor, and shall return to his own land; and I will cause him to fall by the sword in his own land.

In 2 Kings 19:35, it says the angel of the Lord smote the camp of the Assyrians. God brought His word to pass because Hezekiah prayed for help. Hezekiah learns from this situation that God keeps His word because Hezekiah saw his enemy destroyed as God had said.

In 2 Kings 20, Isaiah tells Hezekiah to set his house in order because he was going to die. When the prophet leaves Hezekiah prays and weeps before God. God then changes His mind and sends Isaiah back to tell Hezekiah he will be healed in three days. Hezekiah then asks for sign that this is true. He asks the prophet for something impossible in the natural. He tells Isaiah the sign he wants is for the shadow to go back ten degrees on the sun dial. This instrument was used to tell time during Hezekiah's time. Time would have to stop in order for this to happen. Isaiah prayed and the Lord caused the shadow to go back ten degrees. I believe God was trying to show Hezekiah that there was a more powerful place that Hezekiah could reach by using Isaiah as an example. However, Hezekiah did have power with God in that in this instance God changed His mind and reversed His word. Abraham had this type of relationship with God in that God changed His mind concerning Sodom and Gomorrah. Hezekiah knew that God kept His word, but in this instance God changed His mind because of their relationship.

The next situation in Hezekiah's life was when he showed the King of Babylon his riches. God became angry with Hezekiah because of pride. I believe Hezekiah became lukewarm as the Laodicea church in Revelation 3:14. God said to that church that they were lukewarm because they said they were rich, and increased with goods, and have need of nothing; and they did not know that they were wretched, and miserable, and poor, and blind and naked. God tells them to buy from Him gold tried in the fire. Gold in the natural is one of the most precious things to have. In God's kingdom the most precious item is love. God wanted the Laodicea church to allow Him to perfect their love. This happens by denying yourself and bearing your cross daily. God was trying to get Hezekiah to come up higher to get closer to the Lord.

Isaiah comes to Hezekiah and said all that is in his house will be taken to Babylon. He also said his sons will be taken to Babylon and become eunuchs in the palace of the King of Babylon. Hezekiah's response is seen in II Kings 20:19.

It says:

> *Then said Hezekiah unto Isaiah, Good is the word of the Lord which thou hast spoken. And he said, Is it not good, if peace and truth be in my days?*

Here was a man in the glory of God. This was a man that changed God's mind through his prayer yet he got satisfied and was in pride. When the word came about his children he forgot that prayer could have changed God's mind. When he said the word was good, Hezekiah was only thinking of himself. He did not impart to His children the blessing of a close relationship with God. God wanted Hezekiah to go from glory to glory. Isaiah was to be an example for him that there was a greater glory. There was no king closer to God than Hezekiah, but God wanted him to go higher. I believe Isaiah was closer to God in that when he prayed the earth stopped so time would go back. The Scripture shows that David was the father of Hezekiah. David's legacy went to his children but Hezekiah did not cry out for his children. God wants us to come into glory so that His kingdom will touch or affect the earth. Isaiah was a man that affected the earth. He prayed and the earth stopped. God's glory is not just for us but it is so we can affect our families, friends, church, the earth and bring glory to God.

Romans 8:18-19 says:

18.

For I reckon that the sufferings of this present time are not worthy to be compared to the glory which shall be revealed in us.

19.

For the earnest expectation of the creature waits for the manifestation of the sons of God.

Hezekiah's example shows us that no matter what your testimony is or how far in glory you are, we must always ask the Father what is next. His glory is like an ocean where there is no end to it. Our prayer must be: Lord, take me beyond the glory of God.

Chapter 8

CONCLUSION: KNOWING YOU ARE IN THE GLORY OF GOD

There came a time in my life when I wondered if glory was with me. "How do you know if glory has come?" was my question. Glory comes when Jesus and the Father come and manifest themselves to you (John 14: 20-23). Abiding with God is knowing that the Father and Jesus are always with you. It is not about how much I pray, but it is having the revelation that He is always there. Paul said, "And be found in Him, not having mine own righteousness, which is of the law, but that which is through the faith of Christ, the righteousness which is of God by faith"(Philippians 3:9). Paul came to understand that the Father and Jesus were with him. It was not because of his prayer life or works, but it was because of the cross.

The Lord over time through Him speaking to me and giving me visions showed me that glory had come in my life. God may let you know by revelation or by another method. The way He shows one may be different than for someone else. Do not compare your experience to someone else's experience. There may be times you have a vision or you may feel His presence with you. In Luke 24:32, there were disciples who were walking with Jesus after He died. At first they did not recognize Him. After He left they said," Did not our heart burn within us, while He talked with us." There will be times you know He is there because your heart burns within you.

There were also times when I felt I blew it and glory was gone. If we sin there is a separation between us and God; however, in order to come back into His presence we need to ask for forgiveness, and know that the blood of Jesus cleanses us from all sin.

I John 1:7 says:

> But if we walk in the light (glory), as He is in the light (glory), we have fellowship one with another, and the blood of Jesus Christ his Son cleanseth us from all sin.

The priests always went into the Holy of Holies with the blood and asked for forgiveness. In the same way, when we find ourselves out of His presence we are to ask for forgiveness and continue to walk with Him. God wants us to stay away from sin so we can walk in confidence knowing that He is with us. Sin causes a veil of unbelief to come on us and we may not even know it. This is what happened to the children of Israel (2 Corinthians 3: 14 – 16).

How do you know if you have the glory? I believe 2 Chronicles 15:2 has the answer.

> *Hear ye me Asa, and all Judah and Benjamin; the Lord is with you, while you be with Him; and if ye seek Him, He will be found of you; but if you forsake Him, He will forsake you.*

It is that simple, He is with you while you are with Him. The Lord will never leave us because of love.

John also gives us insight into this in I John 2:3-6:

3.

> *And hereby we do know that we know Him, if we keep His commandments.*

4.

> *He that saith, I know Him, and keeps not His commandments, is a liar, and the truth is not in Him.*

5.

> *But whoso keeps His word, in Him verily is the love of God perfected: hereby know we that we are in Him.*

6.

> *He that saith **He abideth in Him** ought himself so walk, even as He walked.*

We know we are in him when we deny ourselves and keep His commandments. When we know He is with us, we do not want to offend Him, and we do not want to hurt Him. It is a place of faith and not works. This faith comes by the Lord telling you that you are in love, in His heart. II Chronicles 7: 14-16, says for those that seek Him His eyes and heart will be with them perpetually. That means His heart will be with them forever. When the Lord brings you into His heart He does not put you out. This is when 2 Corinthians 5:14, becomes real in that His love constrains us and keeps us from sinning against Him. We will find that He is able to keep us from falling and bring us faultless before the presence of His glory (Jude24).

Hebrews 1:2-3 shows that Jesus is the kingdom, power and glory. In verse 3, it says that Jesus is *the brightness of His glory*. When we know Jesus has come and is with us we can conclude that His glory is with us. Whenever God showed His glory what did these individuals see? They saw one who was like the Son of man. They saw Jesus.

When I know Jesus is with me, which is faith, then I know that the power of God is with me also. Isaiah 40:10 says that when He comes, He comes with power.

When Jesus comes, He is the kingdom of God. This is because He is an heir of God and is set down at the right hand of God the Father. All things are under His feet and He has all power and authority. Jesus said in Matthew 12:28, "That if He cast out devils by the Spirit of God then the kingdom of God is come unto you." He is the kingdom, power and glory.

John 14: 21-23 showed us that when we keep His commandments we love Him and the Father and Son will come and manifest themselves to us and make their abode with us. This is when we know glory has come. This is when faith is birthed and we walk in Him. This is when we walk in perfect oneness. The Lord showed me perfect oneness is like me being a molecule of water in an ocean, the ocean being God. Paul says in I Corinthians 6:17, "But he that is joined to the Lord is one spirit." When He comes to me glory has come, and He wants to take me from glory to glory.

A friend of mine, Barb Knight says, "That when glory or His presence comes what is His purpose?" Experiencing God's glory is not the end but just the beginning. The Lord wants us to go beyond the glory of God to experience His kingdom within us. Beyond the glory is realizing all that is mine in the kingdom.

In conclusion I leave you with Psalms 91:1:

> He that dwelleth in the secret place of the Most High shall abide **under the shadow of the Almighty.**

Glory is like God's shadow, but His shadow is a shadow of light. Within the light of God is life, within His light is fruit, and within His light is victory.

Revelation 21:11 says:

> Having the glory of God: and her light was like unto a stone most precious, even **like a jasper stone, clear as crystal**

May God bless you to go from glory to glory, and may you inherit His kingdom and dominion. Glory is not the end but just the beginning; it leads us to the Father and Jesus Christ our Lord. Lord, take us beyond the glory of God.

God bless,

Rick Rannie

Pastor Rick Rannie is available for ministry at your church, or conferences. He can be contacted at the following address:

634 Southgate Dr
State College PA 16801

Telephone - 814 404 3065
Email – rannieglory@yahoo.com

Notes

Notes

Notes

Notes

CPSIA information can be obtained at www.ICGtesting.com
Printed in the USA
BVOW040750020512

289167BV00003B/31/P